The 4 dimensions of Love

STUDY IN THE LIGHT OF THE HOLY SCRIPTURES

Essential Collection

The 4 dimensions of Love

STUDY IN THE LIGHT OF THE HOLY SCRIPTURES

JEROME
POULIOT

with the
collaboration of

YVES MALO

Essential Collection

The 4 Dimensions Of Love (N° 003-T4DOL)
Copyright © 2013 Éditions Sous Tes Ailes
Upton (Quebec), Canada

Email: editeur@EditionsSousTesAiles.com
Website: www.EditionsSousTesAiles.com

Desktop Publishing, graphic design and translation: Yves Malo
Reading committee: Daniel Doucet, Denyse Gosselin
Book Cover: © Charon | Dreamstime.com / Sarah O'Neal
Printed in the United States of America

ISBN 978-2-9811957-1-5
Legal Deposit - BanQ - Bibliothèque et Archives nationales du Québec, 2013
Legal Deposit - Library and Archives Canada, 2013

Dédication

This book appears to honor Him whom we have so often despised, abandoned, rejected, disdained, and we have made him no means, as said the prophet Isaiah. The very one who was Love, was not loved or received in this low world. This book pays tribute to Him, for He is The Man who brought love in the affairs of this world. Without Him, this book would not exist, because it does not refer to a selfish love, romantic or passenger. He was Love. He demonstrated that God himself was willing to do to save mankind. No other one has acted or talked like Him.

That is why I want to dedicate this book, Him:

Jesus
of Nazareth !

Contents

Foreword

"When I think of all this, I fall to my knees and pray to the Father, the Creator of everything in heaven and on earth. I pray that from his glorious, unlimited resources he will empower you with inner strength through his Spirit. Then Christ will make his home in your hearts as you trust in him. Your roots will grow down into God's love and keep you strong. And may you have the power to understand, as all God's people should, how wide, how long, how high, and how deep his love is. May you experience the love of Christ, though it is too great to understand fully. Then you will be made complete with all the fullness of life and power that comes from God. Now all glory to God, who is able, through his mighty power at work within us, to accomplish infinitely more than we might ask or think."
Éphesians 3:14-20 (NLT)

To know and live God's love even in its most extensive dimensions, that is the proper to the child of God. It does not speak here about our love to us, but of the love God had for us, and has yet to each of his own. Discover that love, gives us to experiment and become a carrier and a diffuser. The one who can help us taste this love is the very one who spreads it in us because of the work of Jesus Christ.

"Now hope does not disappoint, because the love of God has been poured out in our hearts by the Holy Spirit who was given to us. " Romans 5.5

God's love for us is so great, that he sent someone to transform us personally. This person is always at our side, it is the Holy Spirit. He is the one who both comforts us, teaches us in the truth, leads us, counsels us, strengthens us, transforms us... He transmits to us this great love that is in the heart of the Father, manifested through the work of his son Christ Jesus.

"However, when He, the Spirit of truth, has come, He will guide you into all truth; for He will not speak on His own authority, but whatever He hears He will speak; and He will tell you things to come. He will glorify Me, for He will take of what is Mine and declare it to you. All things that the Father has are Mine. Therefore I said that He will take of Mine and declare it to you. " John 16.13-15

Yves Malo

Introduction

How to define God's love? Can it be compared to human compassion, which consists in helping his fellow man when he goes through a difficult situation? Is it just to reach to the needy, to mourn with those who weep and carry the burdens of one another? While all this is laudable, God sees things very differently than we, his gaze penetrates not only the present, but all eternity. The divine compassion always walk together with his righteousness: they never contradict one and other.

The problem that resides within this "human compassion" is that in its desire to comfort the miserable, it misses the real cause of the fundamental problem of man. In doing so, it takes the party of the sinner that refuses to recognize his personal responsibility, to justify it on his childhood or his environment, "the system", etc. Therefore, by doing this, it avoids to talk about sin to not guilty in order the person you wish to help. How can you cure a problem, such as a disease, if you at first refused to recognize its existence? No patient wants to receive a cure before he recognized the fact that he is sick. But sin is a disease much worse than cancer, which is fatal, and incurable sin poisons all human existence; only the blood of the Lamb erases all traces.

As an ostrich who hides its head in the sand and deny the existence of her problem, that attitude in no way solves the situation. Rather, it is better to look things in front and admit that for humans, it is impossible to avoid the power of sin excepts only by the salvation offered in Christ Jesus. God sees our sin as something grave, very serious, it has long stated that these consequences could only be death.

"but of the tree of the knowledge of good and evil you shall not eat, for in the day that you eat of it you shall surely die. " Genesis 2:17

We never see God saying to man: "Ah, you have sinned... it does not really matter. I understand you, we forget all this and I forgive you!" The world would have us believe this lie, but the divine reality remains otherwise.

"For the wages of sin is death [...] *"* Romans 6:23

God would not grant us the kind of compassion that we could simply exercise to one of our fellow man as the requirements of justice could not be met or satisfied.

Chapter 1

The Width

The attempt on the adamical life

The width of His love talks about the royal largesse (generosity) that God has kindly agreed to graciously pour out on us in Christ Jesus. It is as though God had widened his heart to include us in His eternal plan, despite the fact we have already missed the first time. Adam's fall reached the whole human race and distanced us from the divine presence.

"Therefore, just as through one man sin entered the world, and death through sin, and thus death spread to all men, because all sinned." Romans 5:12

Yet it is precisely then that the largesse of God's love comes touching us in this sinful nature inherited from Adam, Jesus Christ came to our rescue. He took form in a body like our own in order to help us at our level.

"Inasmuch then as the children have partaken of flesh and blood, He Himself likewise shared in the same, that through death He might destroy him who had the power of death, that is, the devil, and release those who through fear of death were all their lifetime subject to bondage. "
Hebrew 2:14-15

Being made like us he has kindly brought upon himself the weight and guilt of our sin by undergoing our condemnation.

"For He made Him who knew no sin to be sin for us, that we might become the righteousness of God in Him. " II Corinthians 5:21

This management of our sinful nature was made just before going to the cross. We find a representation of this fact in what Aaron the high priest had to do in order to receive atonement for the sins of the people: he had to offer not one but two goats as sacrifice.

"He shall take the two goats and present them before the Lord at the door of the tabernacle of meeting. Then Aaron shall cast lots for the two

goats: one lot for the Lord and the other lot for the scapegoat. And Aaron shall bring the goat on which the Lord's lot fell, and offer it as a sin offering. But the goat on which the lot fell to be the scapegoat shall be presented alive before the Lord, to make atonement upon it, and to let it go as the scapegoat into the wilderness. " Leviticus 16:7-10

Note this well: a goat was used to make atonement before the LORD and the other goat to Azazel. Intriguing is it not! Yet the picture is simple and clear.

"The soul who sins shall die. [...] " Ezekiel 18:20

The first goat was to make atonement and therefore, both coverage and substitute for sin in itself. In reality this first goat would suffer the punishment for our sin and would become an inherent part of our nature. Aaron had, in no way, to confess the sins of the people in a personal way and detailed as he should do for the second goat. This first sacrifice covered our sinful nature and God's wrath prevented from reaching us because it fell on the animal substitute. This is what happened initially with Christ; he is dead for our sin as a substitute, first with the nature of sin upon him. But Christ did not remain there, he also had to remove the personal consequences and detail of sin in the everyday life. This is why Aaron took the second live goat and did as follows:

"Aaron shall lay both his hands on the head of the live goat, confess over it all the iniquities of the children of Israel, and all their transgressions, concerning all their sins, putting them on the head of the goat, and shall send it away into the wilderness by the hand of a suitable man. The goat shall bear on itself all their iniquities to an uninhabited land; and he shall release the goat in the wilderness. " Leviticus 16:21-22

It simply meant that God did not just want "*to cover our sin*" but truly erase it once for all, also by taking away from us all trespasses, consequences generated by sin: hatred, fear, bondage, trouble, curses...

"He will again have compassion on us, and will subdue our iniquities. You will cast all our sins into the depths of the sea. " Micah 7:19

This is a complete work of justification that Christ has accomplished at the cross, and not only of forgiveness. Because he has taken the very nature of sin and all its filthy consequences, he brought this to the cross to give us in exchange a new life. For he does not leave the house empty; if he removes something he replaces it by an entirely new nature, his own nature.

"Then I will sprinkle clean water on you, and you shall be clean; I will cleanse you from all your filthiness and from all your idols. I will give you a new heart and put a new spirit within you; I will take the heart of stone out of your flesh and give you a heart of flesh " Ezekiel 36:25-26

This is where God proves his love by expanding his tent and his dwelling down to us, so that we may become ourselves a tent and a dwelling place of God and all of this out of pure grace. The origin and the nature of our first ancestor, Adam, has determined the nature of all who would follow thereafter. However, when Jesus came, he broke this cycle because he started in himself a new creation, a new race of man.

"And because you belong to him, the power of the life-giving Spirit has freed you from the power of sin that leads to death. " Romans 8:2 (NLT)

"Therefore, if anyone is in Christ, he is a new creation; old things have passed away; behold, all things have become new. Now all things are of God, who has reconciled us to Himself through Jesus Christ, and has given us the ministry of reconciliation. " II Corinthians 5:17-18

God is the author of the first creation but the origin and the starting model for all who would follow was Adam, a man became a sinner. However, Christ appeared to begin a new line of man modeled after Himself.

"God knew what he was doing from the very beginning. He decided from the outset to shape the lives of those who love him along the same lines as the life of his Son. The Son stands first in the line of humanity he restored. We see the original and intended shape of our lives there in Him. " Romans 8:29 (TM)

As the Apostle Paul explains several times, Christ is both the last and the new Adam:

"The Scriptures tell us, "The first man, Adam, became a living person." But the last Adam — that is, Christ — is a life-giving Spirit." I Corinthians 15:45 (NLT)

"The first man was of the earth, made of dust; the second Man is the Lord from heaven. As was the man of dust, so also are those who are made of dust; and as is the heavenly Man, so also are those who are heavenly." I Corinthians 15:47-48

Christ is called here the last Adam, for it was he who had ended the first creation of tainted sin. Having accomplished all that was required by the Law, he was able to terminate the natural character of sin which constantly reproduced from father to son. This is how he started a new race of man which contains new "spiritual genes". In him, we are truly recreated, regenerated; a new nature and new characters are now attributed by him to us.

"For you have been born again, but not to a life that will quickly end. Your new life will last

forever because it comes from the eternal, living word of God. " I Peter 1:23 (NLT)

From the same Word which created the first race of people taken from Adam, of this same Word, henceforth, is taken a new line carrying the nature of Christ.

"Whoever has been born of God does not sin, for His seed remains in him; and he cannot sin, because he has been born of God. " I John 3:9

The new birth

Many christians have a wrong idea of what is really the new birth. Several identify the new birth with the fact that the Holy Spirit has come into their lives. However, this is not entirely accurate; as always, the Holy Spirit is there, present, deeply touching the human heart like David, who under his inspiration wrote such beautiful psalms. Certainly with Jesus, the Holy Spirit would come to a greater degree on all believers and with a power never before experienced. The key basis is not only the coming of the Holy Spirit but God had promised to give us a new heart and a new spirit (Ezekiel 36:26), by initially circumcising our heart first. To give us a new heart he had to remove first the old one because no one can live with two hearts within him. This is why Christ exercised a circumcision of the heart, carrying with him in his death our old nature sold under sin, that had put its hold within our own spirit.

"For we know that the law is spiritual, but I am carnal, sold under sin. " Romans 7:14

"In Him you were also circumcised with the circumcision made without hands, by putting off the body of the sins of the flesh, by the circumcision of Christ, buried with Him in baptism, in which you also were raised with Him through faith in the working of God, who raised Him from the dead. " Colossians 2:11-12

It is important to understand this: Eve was taken from Adam, she is somehow born of him, not by natural course, but by divine surgical intervention that has made her, as it is written in the Word of God: "*bone of my bones and flesh of my flesh*" (Genesis 2:23). We ourselves have been taken from Christ because we are His Bride. We were born from Him by divine surgical intervention, and we became "*spirit of his Spirit, body from His Body*". It is exactly this new birth: we receive a new spirit from Christ as the same essence. This was made possible because Christ first extracted the old spirit "*corrupted by sin*" by nailing it at the cross with him. We can also see a beautiful image of this in the fact that the side of Jesus was pierced just below his ribs (John 19:34). God has also had to pierce Adam for him to remove a rib to create Eve his wife; for this purpose, God made Adam fall into a deep sleep (Genesis 2:23). Similarly, Jesus had to pass through the sleep of death so that his Father could remove one of his ribs and create the new Church, the Bride of Christ.

We have been recreated from Jesus, from his body, bruised and pierced. Jesus' death was necessary to bring the final and fatal stroke to the old breath (spirit) which made us all corrupt. From his nature and his essence we came back to life with Christ, resurrected to a new life. The child that leaves the womb actually dies to his old environment, its former way of life and existence culminating in a whole new life. Thus it was with us: we have ceased to live within the Adamic matrix which had been defiled by sin; now live in the open air of the Spirit of God. This new spirit born of the very nature of Christ is still a newborn, which is why he is placed under the direct control of the Holy Spirit which acts as a mother. This is also the Holy Spirit who is the agent incubator of this new spirit in us by allowing the glory of Christ to reach us. Jesus Christ actually becomes our new Adam, the father of all living creatures in Christ which now shall rise to a new life through faith in Him.

"And He is the head of the body, the church, who is the beginning, the firstborn from the dead, that in all things He may have the preeminence." Colossians 1:18

You see, it is important to fully understand what the Scripture says about the new birth. For it is in our inheritance to know that Christ has really initiated a new nature in us, his own nature which is no longer subjected to sin.

"But you are not in the flesh but in the Spirit, if indeed the Spirit of God dwells in you. Now if anyone does not have the Spirit of Christ, he is not His. And if Christ is in you, the body is dead because of sin, but the Spirit is life because of righteousness." Romans 8:9-10

It really is a new reality that can make all the difference in our lives because it refers to a justice that was given to us by God from above, entirely free of charge that has nothing to do with our own righteousness.

"For the kingdom of God is not eating and drinking, but righteousness and peace and joy in the Holy Spirit. " Romans 14:17

God calls us to live not as a desolate widow who is still fighting against sin but as a bride, who is highly graced and that benefits from the very nature of Christ which is fully victorious over sin. We only need to fully seize it by faith and live with what has been provided at the cross of Christ. For it is to that extent that the generosity of God went, a legacy to the height of God's love which surpasses all knowledge.

One last interesting detail concerning the new birth relates to where we need to go through to reach this new life. Indeed, the newborn must pass through the narrow passage of the womb before coming into this new life. We also are required to pass through a narrow passage, where we must leave behind our entire life if we want to inherit this new life. The Adamic life, defiled and corrupted by sin, can not follow through this narrow pass and must be left behind. Losing his life to Jesus is really finding it back. Wanting to keep it, still looking to improve it is to lose the power of Jesus to deliver us forever from this sinful nature. As long as human pride still believes that there is something good in his life, he will refuse to lose it in the hands of Jesus. If, on the contrary, we recognize that there is nothing good in us, that our life is a complete failure because of sin, it will be easy for us to abandon it in his hands in order to rise with him into a new life.

"Yet indeed I also count all things loss for the excellence of the knowledge of Christ Jesus my Lord, for whom I have suffered the loss of all things, and count them as rubbish, that I may gain Christ and be found in Him, not having my own righteousness, which is from the law, but that which is through faith in Christ, the righteousness which is from God by faith. " Philippians 3:8-9

United in His death and resurrection

As the Apostle Paul often explains, this new nature begins as a newborn and requires growth. As a baby, it needs to be constantly nourished by the faith that comes from the Word of God, to grow and develop in all areas of our lives. At all points, this spirit is modeled on Jesus Christ, for in essence it is born of Him. Our union with Christ becomes complete in every sense of the word, as in his death and resurrection.

"Or do you not know that as many of us as were baptized into Christ Jesus were baptized into His death? Therefore we were buried with Him through baptism into death, that just as Christ was raised from the dead by the glory of the Father, even so we also should walk in newness of life. For if we have been united together in the likeness of His death, certainly we also shall be in the likeness of His resurrection, knowing this, that our old man was crucified with Him, that the body of sin might be done away with, that we should no longer be slaves of sin. For he who has died has been freed from sin. " Romans 6:3-7

This is what Paul also explains in the Epistle to the Galatians:

"For I through the law died to the law that I might live to God. I have been crucified with Christ ; it is no longer I who live, but Christ lives in me ; and the life which I now live in the flesh I live by faith in the Son of God, who loved me and gave Himself for me. " Galatians 2:19-20

Think about it! God does not do things halfway: if He began in us a new creation its that He has already put to death what was beforehand. The former condition is outdated. What we once were has disappeared. The new creation has already begun, behold: everything has become new (II Corinthians 5:17-18). Jesus is really "*the firstborn among many brethren*" (Romans 8:29), therefore, is that all who follow thereafter are called to be like him in every way. Likewise, know that Jesus had a human nature in him undefiled by sin as well, newborns that he recreates in his image also possess a regenerated human nature not tainted by sin. On the other hand, this new nature will require more and more to grow and to invade our minds and thoughts. There is a whole part of us that needs adjusting with this new spirit.

Indeed, if we have been regenerated at the level of our spirit, soul and body, however, retain some traces left (residues) by sin. It still affects our feelings, our will and our intellect so that, by force of habit, it can be easy for the devil to bring us back to our old life. It is essential that our faith remains firm against the attacks of the enemy in order not to be shaken as to the work already accomplished by Christ.

"Be sober, be vigilant; because your adversary the devil walks about like a roaring lion, seeking whom he may devour. Resist him, steadfast in the faith, knowing that the same sufferings are experienced by your brotherhood in the world."
I Peter 5:8-9

The truth of the Word will provide a firm faith in this new creation placed in me by Christ Jesus. Moreover, it will renew our minds so that our soul is cleansed of any bad memories. So the Word of God will become like pure water which cleanses the conscious parts of my being (my soul) of the memory of sin. At the same time it sheds light on the new paths that my regenerated spirit is led to explore. The Holy Spirit administers all this as a gentle overseer; It ensures that its implementation and speech becomes its own as an offensive weapon of the most dangerous to counter the attacks that may occur.

"For though we walk in the flesh, we do not war according to the flesh. For the weapons of our warfare are not carnal but mighty in God for pulling down strongholds, casting down arguments and every high thing that exalts itself against the knowledge of God, bringing every thought

thought into captivity to the obedience of Christ. " II Corinthians 10:3-5 (NLT)

It is as if one wished to implement a new machine in a factory, then the employees would need time to relearn how to operate in this new environment. It is the same with us, we need to be constantly renewed in our minds by the truth, to relearn how to live according to the heavenly pattern. This is the work of the Holy Spirit in us, but we must take part continually by cultivating an intimate relationship with the Lord. Prayer, reading the Word of God, praise and worship are all assets used by the Spirit of God to prompt us to the renewal of our mind.

"If then you were raised with Christ, seek those things which are above, where Christ is, sitting at the right hand of God. Set your mind on things above, not on things on the earth. For you died, and your life is hidden with Christ in God. " Colossians 3:1-3

This is how the Holy Spirit can lead us into the paths he has traced out in advance for us. Having explored the width of God's love which extends to remove this adamic nature from us to put in its place, we may also find that by doing this, God the

Father could adopt us as sons and daughters. Now we are raised to the position occupied by his own royal son, Jesus.

"For if by the one man's offense death reigned through the one, much more those who receive abundance of grace and of the gift of righteousness will reign in life through the One, Jesus Christ. " Romans 5:17

The expectation of the Bridegroom to the Bride

"[...] Christ also loved the church and gave Himself for her, that He might sanctify and cleanse her with the washing of water by the word, that He might present her to Himself a glorious church, not having spot or wrinkle or any such thing, but that she should be holy and without blemish. " Ephesians 5:25-27

Christ wants us at his side. He wants to raise our hearts and our thoughts to heavenly things, for that we savored who he is for us and everything he did. As a bride in love with him, he expects from us a whole heart to love him, follow him regardless of the vexations of life. The Psalms describe very well the relationship that exists between the believer and his Saviour.

"Whom have I in heaven but You? And there is none upon earth that I desire besides You. My flesh and my heart fail; But God is the strength of my heart and my portion forever. For indeed, those who are far from You shall perish; You have destroyed all those who desert You for harlotry. But it is good for me to draw near to God; I have put my trust in the Lord GOD, That I may declare all Your works. " Psalm 73:25-28

In the original hebrew text, the expression *"those who desert You"* refers to those who prostitute themself, that commit adultery with someone else. God wants us wholly to him; he can not bear spiritual adultery. He wants us near him, near his heart, close to him as a husband in heaven. He has done everything to make this possible, but it's still up to us the liberty of replying to his call and choosing to live very close to him.

"You're cheating on God. If all you want is your own way, flirting with the world every chance you get, you end up enemies of God and his way. And do you suppose God doesn't care? The proverb has it that "he's a fiercely jealous lover." And what he gives in love is far better than anything else you'll find. " James 4.4-5 (TM)

If such strong words as "cheating", "flirting", "lover", "fiercely jealous" are used, it really means that God puts great emphasis on the intimate relationship we have with him. Christ's death on the cross has provided for the complete and final deliverance from the power of sin in us, and he has completely freed the way to make us like him, "flesh of his flesh", "spirit of his Spirit." But even after having done so much for us, he will not force our love towards him. We remain free to cherish him in return, or be overwhelmed by the cares and concerns of this world. His grace is never something irresistible; precisely, because it is gracious, it expects a positive reply, free and voluntary on our part to live up to what Christ has done for us. It is up to us to choose, knowing for sure that what Christ offers us there is nothing comparable in the world. His love is so great and so marvelous, it would be foolish not to get caught by such grace. The psalmist warns us again in this same psalm that was mentioned earlier, not to let our eyes be enticed by things of this world, not to be seduced by Satan, the great enemy of our souls.

"Truly God is good to Israel, To such as are pure in heart. But as for me, my feet had almost stumbled; My steps had nearly slipped. For I was

envious of the boastful, When I saw the prosperity of the wicked. " Psalm 73:1-3

"When I thought how to understand this, It was too painful for me — Until I went into the sanctuary of God; Then I understood their end." Psalm 73:16-17

We need to learn to find all our joy and happiness in Christ and not let visible things around us, turn away our eyes from him. Do not look at visible things but on what is unseen (II Corinthians 4:18); Let us sit down with Christ in the heavenly places (Ephesians 2:6), where we were transported by faith.

"Giving thanks to the Father who has qualified us to be partakers of the inheritance of the saints in the light. He has delivered us from the power of darkness and conveyed us into the kingdom of the Son of His love. " Colossians 1:12-13

The Heavenly Bridegroom could soon act towards his Bride, who day and night, fixed, her eyes on Him! The royal largesse of our Bridegroom is so majestic that He is worthy to receive from us all praise, all love, all thanksgiving and of course, our entire faithfulness.

"For I am jealous for you with godly jealousy. For I have betrothed you to one husband, that I may present you as a chaste virgin to Christ." II Corinthians 11:2

Before being able to claim that his power is manifested on us, we must learn to live and find in him all our joy, knowing that he is the source of our life.

"Both the singers and the players on instruments say, "All my springs are in you. " " Psalm 87:7

"Then I will go to the altar of God, To God my exceeding joy; And on the harp I will praise You, O God, my God!" Psalm 43:4

His altar, where Christ died for us is also where we find our old nature and receive His own. All our inheritance is there hidden in him. Here at the cross also opens for us the second dimension of His love that we will explore in the next chapter.

Chapter 2

The Length

Much more than forgiveness

Who says length says longanimity, and who says longanimity also says patience!

"And the Lord passed before him and proclaimed, "The Lord, the Lord God, merciful and gracious, longsuffering, and abounding in goodness and truth, keeping mercy for thousands, forgiving iniquity and transgression and sin, by no means clearing the guilty, visiting the iniquity of the fathers upon the children and the children's children to the third and the fourth generation.""
Exodus 34:6-7

Is it not amazing that God, yet so patient, takes the time to mention that he does not clear the guilty even while speaking of forbearance, forgiveness and goodness. If there is forgiveness, it is precisely that the guilty is now considered innocent. Do you not find it strange that something seems to contradict this statement coming from the mouth of God? If he does not clear the guilty, then who can be forgiven? For the Bible is very clear:

"For all have sinned and fall short of the glory of God." Romans 3:23

The apostle Paul explains this apparent dilemma by stating that the culprit was never acquitted, or that God has forgotten our fault or ignored it. In reality, it is rather because the chastisements that we deserved have struck someone else, another has been punished on our behalf, Christ himself as substitute.

"For God presented Jesus as the sacrifice for sin. People are made right with God when they believe that Jesus sacrificed his life, shedding his blood. This sacrifice shows that God was being fair when he held back and did not punish those who sinned in times past, for he was looking ahead and including them in what he would do in this present time. God did this to demonstrate his righteousness, for he himself is fair and just, and he declares sinners to be right in his sight when they believe in Jesus." Romans 3:25-26 (NLT)

This is consistent with what had been said by the prophet Isaiah long ago:

"Surely He has borne our griefs and carried our sorrows; yet we esteemed Him stricken, smitten by God, and afflicted. But He was wounded for our transgressions, He was bruised for our iniquities; the chastisement for our peace was upon Him, and by His stripes we are healed. All we like sheep have gone astray; we have turned, every one, to his own way; and the Lord has laid on Him the iniquity of us all. He was oppressed and He was afflicted, yet He opened not His mouth; He was led as a lamb to the slaughter, and as a sheep before its shearers is silent, so He opened not His mouth. He was taken from prison and from judgment, and who will declare His generation? For He was cut off from the land of the living; for the transgressions of My people He was stricken. " Isaiah 53:4-8

The source of his forbearance is therefore not a "forgiveness" as many people see it, where you simply forget the offense. God has never forgotten the offense, he has instead punished Jesus for our own fault so that it was simply an *act of righteousness* and not an act of mercy. This is where we discover his forbearance in what Christ has accomplished for us. This act of divine righteousness, contrary to what is thought about a simple pardon, covers an infinitely long list of transgressions and direct consequences of our sins. Say first, that his chastisement at the cross extends through the dimension of time to cover not only the present, but also the past as far as we can go back and the future for as long as life is granted to us. For Christ did not leave anything opened. God knew all our sins before we committed them and already he had placed the full punishment on the back of his Son. What love! You no longer have to live in fear of any reproach from God. Everything was brought at the cross. When Jesus appeared after his resurrection to the apostle Peter, who had denied him three times and yet he had no complaints to make against him. This also had been paid at the cross! God's atonement covering covers the entire life time past, present and future. What a great security for our fragile little feelings! What an assurance to counteract this guilt that keeps coming to accuse us and comes from no other than the devil! Of course, I am speaking here to the christians who have believed in Jesus and in his expiatory work at the cross. Without this faith in Him, forgiveness is not even possible before God and so all guilt has access and complete right to the heart of this person. O what treasures of grace become accessible at the altar of the bloody cross of Christ Jesus!

The acquittal of our great debt

Jesus, not only has he suffered the penalty for our sins, past, present and future but he also suffered in himself all possible consequences of sin. The list in this regard is terribly long; sin has left traces on many levels. Lets look briefly at their enumeration and then we will contemplate more the length of his love. At the level of soul, Jesus bore all these horrible feelings which came from sin:

"And among those nations you shall find no rest, nor shall the sole of your foot have a resting place; but there the Lord will give you a trembling heart, failing eyes, and anguish of soul. " Deuteronomy 28:65

- loss of peace: a troubled soul which constantly reproaches himself of things with a sense of guilt and shame at having been taken in the fact;

- a restless heart which constantly fearing the future;

- the languishing eyes, who are desperate of life;

- a suffering soul because of sin which makes her sick, worse than cancer and without Christ, can not heal itself;

- the sin, again, separates us from God and causes us to lose our true reason for living and the joy that follows.

"Your life shall hang in doubt before you; you shall fear day and night, and have no assurance of life. " Deuteronomy 28:66

- *a constant fear, feelings of uncontrollable panic attacks and anguish, personal doubts and individual total uncertainty.*

"In the morning you shall say, 'Oh, that it were evening!' And at evening you shall say, 'Oh, that it were morning!' because of the fear which terrifies your heart, and because of the sight which your eyes see. "And the Lord will take you back to Egypt in ships, by the way of which I said to you,

'You shall never see it again.' And there you shall be offered for sale to your enemies as male and female slaves, but no one will buy you.'"
Deuteronomy 28:67-68

- the feeling of being rejected by all, treated as less than nothing, unworthy to love and be loved.

The soul of Jesus has been literally broken and invaded by all this darkness because at the cross he carried all the curses of our soul which were connected to our sin.

"He was taken from prison and from judgment, And who will declare His generation? For He was cut off from the land of the living; For the transgressions of My people He was stricken. And they made His grave with the wicked — But with the rich at His death, Because He had done no violence, Nor was any deceit in His mouth. Yet it pleased the Lord to bruise Him; He has put Him to grief. When You make His soul an offering for sin, He shall see His seed, He shall prolong His days, And the pleasure of the Lord shall prosper in His hand. He shall see the labor of His soul, and be satisfied. By His knowledge My righteous Servant shall justify many, For He shall bear their

iniquities. Therefore I will divide Him a portion with the great, And He shall divide the spoil with the strong, Because He poured out His soul unto death, And He was numbered with the transgressors, And He bore the sin of many, And made intercession for the transgressors. " Isaiah 53:8-12

"Now My soul is troubled, and what shall I say? 'Father, save Me from this hour?' But for this purpose I came to this hour. " John 12:27

"And He took Peter, James, and John with Him, and He began to be troubled and deeply distressed. Then He said to them, "My soul is exceedingly sorrowful, even to death. Stay here and watch. " " Mark 14:33-34

Jesus knew, because of the darkness that invaded his soul, that he would experience all the punishment for our sins. Yet this darkness that was ours came to surround Him, the Righteous One, so that he would suffer the punishment that we deserved.

"When I was with you daily in the temple, you did not try to seize Me. But this is your hour, and the power of darkness. " Luke 22:53

The long list of our physical punishment
Now Jesus also carried in his own body, the consequences of sins that should have afflicted our bodies. Let's look here at some of the curses which were to reach us, and that of course all due to sin:

- disease in all its forms
  "Then the Lord will bring upon you and your descendants extraordinary plague — great and prolonged plagues — and serious and prolonged sicknesses. Moreover He will bring back on you all the diseases of Egypt, of which you were afraid, and they shall cling to you. Also every sickness and every plague, which is not written in this Book of the Law, will the Lord bring upon you until you are destroyed. " Deuteronomy 28:59-61

- mental illness
  "The Lord will strike you with madness and blindness and confusion of heart. " Deuteronomy 28:28

- famine
  "Because you did not serve the Lord your God with joy and gladness of heart, for the abundance of everything, therefore you

shall serve your enemies, whom the Lord will send against you, in hunger, in thirst, in nakedness, and in need of everything; and He will put a yoke of iron on your neck until He has destroyed you."
Deuteronomy 28:47-48

- curse in all
  "Cursed shall you be in the city, and cursed shall you be in the country. Cursed shall be your basket and your kneading bowl. Cursed shall be the fruit of your body and the produce of your land, the increase of your cattle and the offspring of your flocks. Cursed shall you be when you come in, and cursed shall you be when you go out."
  Deuteronomy 28:16-19

- trouble and threat
  "The Lord will send on you cursing, confusion, and rebuke in all that you set your hand to do, until you are destroyed and until you perish quickly, because of the wickedness of your doings in which you have forsaken Me. " Deuteronomy 28:20

- financial curse
  "The alien who is among you shall rise

higher and higher above you, and you shall come down lower and lower. He shall lend to you, but you shall not lend to him; he shall be the head, and you shall be the tail." Deuteronomy 28:43-44

Those curses affect all areas of our lives and are on the physical level. This is why Jesus also carried in his own body, all the chastisement that our sin deserved.

"When evening had come, they brought to Him many who were demon-possessed. And He cast out the spirits with a word, and healed all who were sick, that it might be fulfilled which was spoken by Isaiah the prophet, saying: He Himself took our infirmities and bore our sicknesses. " Matthieu 8.16-17

"For you know the grace of our Lord Jesus Christ, that though He was rich, yet for your sakes He became poor, that you through His poverty might become rich. " II Corinthians 8:9

As it is mentioned in the book of the prophet Isaiah (53:4-11), Jesus bore our:

- sufferings,

- sorrows,
- sins,
- wandering,
- strokes,
- humiliation,
- wounds,
- brokenness,
- punishment,
- iniquities,
- abuse,
- and yoke.

And if he has bore on our behalf all these things, they now have no reason to be there; the sin no longer has any right to claim any salary:

"For the wages of sin is death, but the gift of God is eternal life in Christ Jesus our Lord."
Romans 6:23

The final and definitive wage of sin on our body should be death. However, Christ also carried it to deliver us forever from its power.

"But we see Jesus, who was made a little lower than the angels, for the suffering of death crowned with glory and honor, that He, by the grace of God, might taste death for everyone."
Hebrew 2:9

The wound of our High Priest

To better understand these first two facets of divine love, lets put them in perspective one beside the other. His love has firslty grown into a royal largesse (abundance), a king who dies for his subjects to become one with Him, and now partakes in His nature. Jesus became man, the King eternal, the Son of God, took our adamic nature corrupted and died on our behalf, as the last Adam leading in his death the destruction of our own sinful nature. Became our new Adam royal and divine, one side is taken from him to recreate us in His image and likeness, spirit of his spirit and body of his body. O what a glorious salvation and most of all what love! Only a perfect king, divine and animated by such a great love could do so, to regenerate a Bride doomed to perdition. He made us his beloved Bride, animated by his own nature. But now, in his great love, Christ extends a forbearance more than ever before. He becomes our High Priest, bearing on himself all the consequences of past, present and future of our sins. Again, if Jesus died only in the same way a lamb is slaughtered for sacrifice, it would have been much. But that's not how Jesus died, he has not suffered a quick death and with few suffering. It was an veritable agony he endured. He supported in himself all the terror pour and shame of being lashed up to forty lashes minus one; then he was subjected to death the longest and most suffering of all, that of the crucifixion.

Why? Because he has not only bore our sins, he also suffered into his flesh every awful and terrible consequences. The expiatory goat that was released in the desert in a land barren and desolate, was destined to die very slowly. This is what Christ passed through, he was not only the first sacrificial goat which was to die for our sins, but he was also the second atoning goat condemned to suffer long before dying.

From Mount of Olives, the Garden of Gethsemane, until his death upon the cross, the bitter herbs have deeply invaded him by the extremes of darkness reached. Pierced with wounds, struck with shame, he suffered the worst of the worst criminals, to whom the crowd would have liked to inflict some suffering of these "alleged victims". Broken, humiliated, anguish, betrayed, abandoned, stripped, abused, cursed and carries our own chastisement *so that the devil never has the right again to claim any punishment for our sins*. Trace is erased forever, it remains absolutely nothing. All stock of our lives under the influence of sin has been erased, as if we had never sinned.

"[…] Look! The Lamb of God who takes away the sin of the world!" John 1:29 (NLT)

Can you stop for a moment, to realize and become aware of the full extent of his love! Nothing here below is worth this love! You will not find anywhere else! Jesus paid a tremendous price for having us, because he loved us. If he did not intervene we were lost, damned. Nobody has ever forced him to do so: it is by purest love, a total gift of self, he gave himself for us.

"Therefore My Father loves Me, because I lay down My life that I may take it again. No one takes it from Me, but I lay it down of Myself. I have power to lay it down, and I have power to take it again. This command I have received from My Father." John 10:17-18

And when he adopted us as his own, he knew he embarked in a huge contract with us! What it cost him is tremendous, but even now every heavenly resources are deployed to perfect this jewel that we are. For his power covers not only our past but also our present and our future. If he has now invested in us His own nature, he has also placed all in preparation for us a plan traced in advance, the works prepared in the image of the Son of God.

"Most assuredly, I say to you, he who believes in Me, the works that I do he will do also; and greater works than these he will do, because I go to My Father. " John 14:12

For if he removes the curse, he also creates the blessing instead. And this is all that remains for our future: the blessing, the blessing yet, and always more blessings, all the more glorious than the others.

"Blessed be the God and Father of our Lord Jesus Christ, who has blessed us with every spiritual blessing in the heavenly places in Christ!" Ephesians 1:3

The curse can no longer exist, if indeed we enter this heavenly reality by faith, and we fully embrace His nature in us. The goodness of our King has led us to inherit his nature, and forbearance to inherit his blessing. Our King has made us a Bride now provided with His own divine and royal nature, and our High Priest has made of us a race of priests destined to fill the earth with the heavenly blessing.

"But you are the ones chosen by God, chosen for the high calling of priestly work, chosen to be a holy people, God's instruments to do his work and speak out for him, to tell others of the night-and-day difference he made for you — from nothing to something, from rejected to accepted. " I Peter 2:9-10 (TM)

" [...] not returning evil for evil or reviling for reviling, but on the contrary blessing, knowing that you were called to this, that you may inherit a blessing. " I Peter 3:9

Much more than a marriage

In Scripture, God has provided several images for his heavenly realities. One of his representations, very precious in symbolism, is found in the fact that God has treated a covenant with us by the blood of the Lamb. First be noted that in an alliance, there was always reciprocal sharing of personal advantages. The brotherly covenant between David and Jonathan was a good example, where goods of one became the property of the other and vice versa.

"Then Jonathan and David made a covenant, because he loved him as his own soul. And Jonathan took off the robe that was on him and gave it to David, with his armor, even to his sword and his bow and his belt. " I Samuel 18:3-4

So Jesus did the same with us; in exchange for our life defiled by sin, he gives us in return his pure and holy life. Our spirit has become his possession, and from his Spirit he breathed in us that belongs to us now. This is much more than simple exchange of vows or promises as in a marriage, which too often in our days ends by a divorce. When Jesus made a covenant with us, he did not only vows, he literally gave his whole life for us.

"Greater love has no one than this, than to lay down one's life for his friends. " John 15:13

"I am the good shepherd. The good shepherd gives His life for the sheep. " John 10:11

The baptism is actually our reciprocal response to this alliance, saying: "*Yes I recognize this extraordinary gift of love that you have done for me. I get your life and to this end, I give you mine too.*" It is a wonderful exchange, where my sin has fallen on Christ and His righteousness came upon me. It was the only way for God, while remaining just to bring us back to life.

"*to demonstrate at the present time His righteousness, that He might be just and the justifier of the one who has faith in Jesus.*" Romans 3:26

Thus, baptism is much more than a vow or a promise to follow him, it is a total self-giving, a liberating exchange, an entrance into alliance where His sinless life comes to dwell in me, and where I abandon mine to him without conditions my whole life contaminated by sin. This is what propels me into a complete transformation of my life.

"*But God, who is rich in mercy, because of His great love with which He loved us, even when we were dead in trespasses, made us alive together with Christ (by grace you have been saved), and raised us up together, and made us sit together in the heavenly places in Christ Jesus, that in the ages to come He might show the exceeding riches of His grace in His kindness toward us in Christ Jesus. For by grace you have been saved through*

faith, and that not of yourselves; it is the gift of God, not of works, lest anyone should boast."
Ephesians 2:4-9

A promise is always difficult to maintain, but it is not so of baptism, which only demonstrate publicly an already accomplished fact at the heart level. It is is my trust in Christ and my recognition of what He did at the cross, that made it all possible. From this same faith, the new sinless life of Christ flows within me.

The Old Covenant had been merely promises to serve God, which soon failed, because of the sinful nature of man. Indeed, a promise is based on the will of man to do well, while this New Covenant and our baptism are based on the faith in the work already accomplished by Christ, the gift of incomparable love. It is is not a promise of obedience that holds this New Covenant, but on receiving a free gift and our affirmative reply to this divine exchange.

"For all have sinned and fall short of the glory of God, being justified freely by His grace through the redemption that is in Christ Jesus."
Romans 3:23-24

Everything is focused on Him and His love, and not on a supposed own strength that makes us able to obey him. All our vain pretensions fly away when we consider that it is precisely the reason that led the Son of God at the cross, our sin, in other words the disobedience or the inability to keep our promise. If this had not been, Jesus would not have needed to die for us on the cross. When I recognize this love so wonderful, through the Word of God that is preached, I can whereas only prostrate and worship this God so admirable. He gave me in exchange for my life of disobedience, a new life, a lively new spirit of His nature. This exchange includes payment of all debts contracted during our former life of sin:

- Instead He provides *"all paths traced in the heart"* Psaumes 84.5;

- *"a road* [...] called the Highway of Holiness [...] *although a fool, shall not go astray"* Isaiah 35:8;

- *"thoughts of peace and not of evil, to give you a future and a hope"* Jeremiah 29:11;

- a plan where *"all things work together for good to those who love God"* Romans 8:28

God has decided for us that the life and works of his son Jesus should be our model in all. At the same time, all the intimacy and open accessibility that Jesus had with his Father, also become our destiny. A glorious future lies before us. Therefore, we are called to thank him for everything, even for tests which become sources of blessings.

"By entering through faith into what God has always wanted to do for us — set us right with him, make us fit for him — we have it all together with God because of our Master Jesus. And that's not all: We throw open our doors to God and discover at the same moment that he has already thrown open his door to us. We find ourselves standing where we always hoped we might stand — out in the wide open spaces of God's grace and glory, standing tall and shouting our praise. There's more to come: We continue to shout our praise even when we're hemmed in with troubles, because we know how troubles can develop passionate patience in us, and how that patience in turn forges the tempered steel of virtue, keeping us alert for whatever God will do next. In alert expectancy such as this, we're never left feeling shortchanged. Quite the contrary — we can't round up enough containers to hold everything God generously pours into our lives through the Holy Spirit!" Romans 5:1-5 (TM)

Chapter 3

The Depth

As wise and deep as his Spirit

Now what about the depth of His love?

"Oh, the depth of the riches and wisdom and knowledge of God! How unfathomable (inscrutable, unsearchable) are His judgments (His decisions)! And how untraceable (mysterious, undiscoverable) are His ways (His methods, His paths)! For who has known the mind of the Lord and who has understood His thoughts, or who has [ever] been His counselor?" Romans 11:33-34 (AB)

"But as it is written: "Eye has not seen, nor ear heard, Nor have entered into the heart of man the things which God has prepared for those who love Him." But God has revealed them to us through His Spirit. For the Spirit searches all things, yes, the deep things of God. For what man knows the things of a man except the spirit of the man which is in him? Even so no one knows the things of God except the Spirit of God. Now we have received, not the spirit of the world, but the Spirit who is from God, that we might know the things that have been freely given to us by God." I Corinthians 2:9-12

His love has grown to us to renew a new life, breathing a new spirit in us the same nature as that of Christ. Then, his forbearance was spilled on all traces left by this life of sin, to erase forever the weight of guilt and even the memory of our sins. But his love would not have been complete, if he had not sent his Spirit to reveal to us the deep ways of God, mysterious, hidden, but intended for those who love him. It is his Spirit that ensures the rooting of the life of Christ in us. As a mother, he oversees every step of her child, ready to extend a hand as soon as he sees the stumbling.

"Rejoice with Jerusalem, And be glad with her, all you who love her; Rejoice for joy with her, all you who mourn for her; That you may feed and be satisfied with the consolation of her bosom, That you may drink deeply and be delighted with the abundance of her glory. For thus says the Lord: Behold, I will extend peace to her like a river, And the glory of the Gentiles like a flowing stream. Then you shall feed; On her sides shall you be carried, And be dandled on her knees. As one whom his mother comforts, So I will comfort you; And you shall be comforted in Jerusalem. The Reign and Indignation of God when you see this, your heart shall rejoice, And your bones shall

flourish like grass; The hand of the Lord shall be known to His servants, And His indignation to His enemies. " Isaiah 66:10-14

It's not in vain and nor coincidence that Jesus himself has called the Holy Spirit: the Comforter.

"I still have many things to say to you, but you cannot bear them now. However, when He, the Spirit of truth, has come, He will guide you into all truth; for He will not speak on His own authority, but whatever He hears He will speak; and He will tell you things to come. " John 16:12-13

"And I will pray the Father, and He will give you another Helper, that He may abide with you forever. " John 14:16

All the Kingdom that Jesus has prepared in advance is only available through the Holy Spirit. It is He who watches to transmit us and to inherit the kingdom.

"Do not fear, little flock, for it is your Father's good pleasure to give you the kingdom. " Luke 12:32

"For the kingdom of God is not eating and drinking, but righteousness and peace and joy in the Holy Spirit. " Romans 14:17

God could not give us better counselor than his own Spirit. We are not left to ourselves, God has not left us to manage by ourself. This is not in the habit from God to do things by half way.

An endless resource

God wanted to take care of everything, so he has not taken the risk to leave us simply an instruction manual by telling us:

"Now, obey what is written!" He knew that the Law did serves to amplify or highlights evil, the nature of sin in us, and that in reality, the Law had led us to die rather than give us the life.

"What shall we say then? Is the law sin? Certainly not! On the contrary, I would not have known sin except through the law. For I would not have known covetousness unless the law had said, "You shall not covet." But sin, taking opportunity by the commandment, produced in me all manner of evil desire. For apart from the law sin was dead. I was alive once without the law, but when

the commandment came, sin revived and I died. And the commandment, which was to bring life, I found to bring death. For sin, taking occasion by the commandment, deceived me, and by it killed me. Therefore the law is holy, and the commandment holy and just and good. Has then what is good become death to me? Certainly not! But sin, that it might appear sin, was producing death in me through what is good, so that sin through the commandment might become exceedingly sinful. For we know that the law is spiritual, but I am carnal, sold under sin. " Romans 7:7-14

God has therefore provided a different way, other than the Law, to lead us today: it is his own Spirit. Here again, it is at the cross that is found the source of this coming of the Spirit. A beautiful image of this is offered to us once more, through the sacrifices that were required by God to obtain full atonement for our sins. In addition to the atoning blood of the goat that was offered on the altar of sacrifice, his fat must also be burned on the fire of the altar.

"The fat of the sin offering he shall burn on the altar. " Leviticus 16:25

This fat, an energy resource of the animal, was torn off and found himself on the altar as a fuel, indeed the fat burns as well as the oil or wood by producing as much energy. Which is to say that the calorific resources of the expiatory goat were now placed at the service of the altar. However there is a picture for us. The Holy Spirit in Christ rendered all his energy and his strength by giving his life; Christ was going to allow his Spirit to be in the service of all who would believe in his expiatory death on the cross (the altar).

"The Spirit of the Lord is upon Me, Because He has anointed Me to preach the gospel to the poor; He has sent Me to heal the brokenhearted, To proclaim liberty to the captives, And recovery of sight to the blind, To set at liberty those who are oppressed; To proclaim the acceptable year of the Lord. " Luke 4:18-19

Which is to say that at the altar, we also had a part in him who is the strength of Christ. His Spirit becomes our energy resource, our heat of everyday, the one that comforts and consoles us like a mother. It is thus that at the cross, Christ has become our wisdom, distributing to each one who believes in his sacrifice, his Spirit. By his blood shed, his life became our life, a new spirit is given to us. But here it is an extra benefit that is added, it is as if our spirit recovers with a thermal protection (fat), his own fat that was on him. It is in this fat burning on the altar that we can distinguish the third dimension of his love. God does not let ourselves be longer wanting of the cold Law and constraining, written on tables of stone. However, no one had ever enough strength to fully observe it.

So Christ, after having solved the problem of sin and its consequences, provides his own Spirit for us that impart (transmit) his divine energy and his capacity to love as He loves us. As a mother brooder that provides of his own heat to warm her chicks and repel the cold outside, so acts the Holy Spirit in us. Assuredly his love is wise and delicate, tender and caring!

"I drew them with gentle cords, With bands of love, And I was to them as those who take the yoke from their neck. I stooped and fed them." Hosea 11:4

His Spirit then becomes like a nourishing mother who provides for our spirit the strength required to grow and fulfill the will of God. In his love, the Lord took charge of everything at the cross, that our salvation is assured and may reach maturity.

"Although my house is not so with God, Yet He has made with me an everlasting covenant, Ordered in all things and secure. For this is all my salvation and all my desire; Will He not make it increase?" II Samuel 23:5

Thank God, for the great love manifested in Christ Jesus! Even fully forgiven and saved, God deliver us not back to the Law. But he handles itself of our education, more tenderly than a mother, giving us his Spirit always present with us. Comprehensive and full of encouragement, his Spirit leads us and guards us against all pitfalls, any obstacle. It is only asked of us to call upon him incessantly while being docile, knowing that He creates in us to will and to do so. Our relationship with him is no longer a *"servile obedience"*, but *"of recognition and love"*. Our submission draws towards him his love, which is why it is not painful (I John 5:3), nor heavy nor difficult (Matthew 11:30).

Penetrate the passion of His love

What is so hard to love the one who loved us so much? The simple fact of meditating on his love, causes us to love him always more, to follow him always more faithfully.

"Let him kiss me with the kisses of his mouth — For your love is better than wine. Because of the fragrance of your good ointments, Your name is ointment poured forth; Therefore the virgins love you. Draw me away! We will run after you. The king has brought me into his chambers. We will be glad and rejoice in you. We will remember your love more than wine. Rightly do they love you.. " Song of Solomon 1:2-4

The mother role exercised by the Holy Spirit, has no other purpose than to lead us to encounter our Bridegroom and our King, Christ, through whom we have been recreated and for whom we are. In reality, we have been delivered from a military discipline to be introduced in a loving relationship with Christ. At the cross, Christ has also nailed this "deadly" Law and he destroyed it.

"having wiped out the handwriting of requirements that was against us, which was

contrary to us. And He has taken it out of the way, having nailed it to the cross. " Colossians 2:14

"So, my dear brothers and sisters, this is the point: You died to the power of the law when you died with Christ. And now you are united with the one who was raised from the dead. As a result, we can produce a harvest of good deeds for God. When we were controlled by our old nature, sinful desires were at work within us, and the law aroused these evil desires that produced a harvest of sinful deeds, resulting in death. But now we have been released from the law, for we died to it and are no longer captive to its power. Now we can serve God, not in the old way of obeying the letter of the law, but in the new way of living in the Spirit. " Romans 7:4-6 (NLT)

So what is being asked of us changes completely. It is no longer required to obey a written law from a book or engraved on tables of stone, but it is required to "*remain united to him*", knowing that his Spirit within us will only lead us to bear much fruit. A loving relationship is what God desires us to grow with him, and not the return to a slavish obedience to the Law. It is face to face, heart to heart, that God wants to walk with us and so to transform us from glory to glory, the image of the stature of Christ.

"who also made us sufficient as ministers of the new covenant, not of the letter but of the Spirit; for the letter kills, but the Spirit gives life." II Corinthians 3:6

"Now the Lord is the Spirit; and where the Spirit of the Lord is, there is liberty. But we all, with unveiled face, beholding as in a mirror the glory of the Lord, are being transformed into the same image from glory to glory, just as by the Spirit of the Lord." II Corinthians 3:17-18

Think a little of all the love that is deployed here by God for us. The same Spirit who was present at the creation of the universe and that moved upon the face over the waters (Genesis 1:2), now he is sent to us, to participate actively and powerfully in this new creation that we are in Christ. The Spirit sees all in advance and every detail, he knows them perfectly. He knows exactly what must be our lives, as it probes the plan that the Father has traced for us. And it is he who monitor the implementation, which is why it is so important for us to love him and give him all our life entirely, and all our decisions.

"O Lord, you have examined my heart and know everything about me. You know when I sit down or stand up. You know my thoughts even when I'm far away. You see me when I travel and when I rest at home. You know everything I do. You know what I am going to say even before I say it, Lord. You go before me and follow me. You place your hand of blessing on my head. Such knowledge is too wonderful for me, too great for me to understand! I can never escape from your Spirit! I can never get away from your presence! If I go up to heaven, you are there; if I go down to the grave, you are there. If I ride the wings of the morning, if I dwell by the farthest oceans, even there your hand will guide me, and your strength will support me. I could ask the darkness to hide me and the light around me to become night — but even in darkness I cannot hide from you. To you the night shines as bright as day. Darkness and light are the same to you. You made all the delicate, inner parts of my body and knit me together in my mother's womb. Thank you for making me so wonderfully complex! Your workmanship is marvelous — how well I know it. You watched me as I was being formed in utter seclusion, as I was woven together in the dark of the womb. You saw me before I was born. Every day of my life was recorded in your book. Every

moment was laid out before a single day had passed. How precious are your thoughts about me, O God. They cannot be numbered! I can't even count them; they outnumber the grains of sand! And when I wake up, you are still with me!" Psalm 139:1-18 (NLT)

This here probably is the best description of the Bible about the depth of God's love. It descends to the innermost parts of our lives to ensure that everything is done according to his will, because he wants the best for us. This is why it is so important to commune every day with his Spirit, to spend time in his presence, to be renewed constantly in our thoughts.

"And do not be conformed to this world, but be transformed by the renewing of your mind, that you may prove what is that good and acceptable and perfect will of God." Romans 12:2

His love will not turn out to be consume into the depths of our being, unless we let him always penetrate us more and more, in a consistent replenished union with His Spirit. His love rendered things so simple and easy; he knew that an enormous code of written laws would have been difficult to observe in all its details. So God sent His own Spirit and we only need now to adhere fully to him, to remain united to him, through the finished work of Christ Jesus at the cross. It's simple, we only have to respond with love, to God's love so deep by his Holy Spirit.

"I love those who love me, And those who seek me diligently will find me. Riches and honor are with me, Enduring riches and righteousness." Proverbs 8:17-18

"Her ways are ways of pleasantness, And all her paths are peace." Proverbs 3:17

"Do not forsake her, and she will preserve you; Love her, and she will keep you." Proverbs 4:6

What was in the Old Covenant, a cold and servile obedience to the commandments written, has become in the New Covenant, a passionate love of his Spirit. This has become an intense and personal love of the living God, who himself lives in us by his Spirit, and that leads to love and to discover more and more our heavenly Bridegroom, Christ. I am convinced that God hates all religious rituals, all forms of monastic abstinences, because He is not at all a God monastery. He is the Creator of nature where everything lives, everything moves, full of joy and liberty. His love is truly in the order of passionate yearning for you and when you taste his divine passion, your heart can only be on fire for him. The divine grace is that the active principle of this love; he gave you his grace in Christ Jesus, because of the work done by his Son, perfect and more than enough. You can not add anything to it, we can only receive it and be completely transformed.

"And of His fullness we have all received, and grace for grace. For the law was given through Moses, but grace and truth came through Jesus Christ. " John 1:16-17

A major problem with the Church today, is not located in terms of what *"she does"* or *"does not do enough"* for his Master, but it's just that She lost her first love. She is no longer on fire for his Lord, as He always is to her. She has left fade away and diminish this flame of love, to fall in the *"we must do this or that"*. God acts toward us only in love, and this is what He wants to receive in return: that we respond unto Him through love, a true love, burning, whole, not just by religious duty. This kind of love receives itself and is primarily lived and then must be:

- preciously preserved
  (I Thessalonicians 5:23);

- kept in its purity (II Timothy 2:22);

- the object of all our affection
  (Colossians 3:2);

- The One toward who our eyes are constantly
  fixed (Hebrew 12:2);

- The One in whom we desire to stay
  (John 15:4).

Our battle is in one of faith, because the object of our desires, Christ, is not seen with our natural eyes. By faith we cherish this love jealously. The One we love has revealed himself to us in spirit and in truth (John 4:24). This actual and tangible reality can not be grasped by our physical senses, but only by our spirit.

"[...] Lord, how is it that You will manifest Yourself to us, and not to the world?" John 14:22

The world can not know him because this latter assimilates only what he sees and hears. But we do know him because He has revealed himself to our heart, and that his love has literally invaded our whole being.

A change of governance

Many christians believe that the main source of their conflicts or their problems comes from the devil, and that they do not observe all the commandments of God. But God does not see things the same perspective, the root cause turns out to be more a problem of governance, inappropriate guidelines and a false confidence. In other words, the problem is at the level of the source of their life, they do not draw their strength at the right place.

"Keep your heart with all diligence, For out of it spring the issues of life. " Proverbs 4:23

Man looks at the outward appearance, all he could do differently to resolve the situation, while God looks at the heart and declares that their source is wrong. They do not place their trust in the right base; they place themselves in their own strength, instead of trusting in God alone and in his work already accomplished at the cross. Why seek to acquire by its own efforts what Christ has already acquired for each of us? He has become our righteousness, our sanctification and our wisdom. Too many of them, look like this poor farmer who is redoubling its efforts to meet his basic needs, on a small plot of land of which he does not know that underground is full of gold. So it is with little children in Christ that still prefer to rely on the crutch of the crippled Law and his good deeds, rather than approach their heavenly Master, and thereby receive from Him gold and all the rich inheritance already deposited in their account.

"Now I say that the heir, as long as he is a child, does not differ at all from a slave, though he is master of all, but is under guardians and stewards until the time appointed by the father. Even so we, when we were children, were in bondage under the elements of the world. But when the fullness of the time had come, God sent forth His Son, born of a woman, born under the law, to redeem those who were under the law, that we might receive the adoption as sons. And because you are sons, God has sent forth the Spirit of His Son into your hearts, crying out, "Abba, Father!" Therefore you are no longer a

slave but a son, and if a son, then an heir of God through Christ. " Galatians 4:1-7

Because it is sad to see that some Christians of little faith think they are still bound by the Law, they find easier to do by themselves instead of relying on what Christ has already accomplished.

"Therefore the law was our tutor to bring us to Christ, that we might be justified by faith. But after faith has come, we are no longer under a tutor. " Galatians 3:24-25

For the faith remains the contact which gives us access to God and all the riches of his grace; it produces in us the love, the peace, the joy, the patience, etc. This entire inheritance is based on the fact that our old sinful nature has been crucified at the cross with Christ, and that it no longer has reason to exist or to claim anything.

"But the fruit of the Spirit is love, joy, peace, longsuffering, kindness, goodness, faithfulness, gentleness, self-control. Against such there is no law. And those who are Christ's have crucified the flesh with its passions and desires. If we live in the Spirit, let us also walk in the Spirit. " Galatians 5:22-25

"So, then, if with Christ you've put all that pretentious and infantile religion behind you, why do you let yourselves be bullied by it? "Don't touch this! Don't taste that! Don't go near this!" Do you think things that are here today and gone tomorrow are worth that kind of attention? Such things sound impressive if said in a deep enough voice. They even give the illusion of being pious and humble and ascetic. But they're just another way of showing off, making yourselves look important. " Colossians 2:20-23 (TM)

Our death in Christ is a reality quite as powerful as the death of Christ himself. By dying, Christ has brought us with him in his death. For those who believe in him, he asserts that his death has also been ours.

"For I through the Law [under the operation of the curse of the Law] have [in Christ's death for me] myself died to the Law and all the Law's demands upon me, so that I may [henceforth] live to and for God. I have been crucified with Christ [in Him I have shared His crucifixion]; it is no longer I who live, but Christ (the Messiah) lives in me; and the life I now live in the body I live by faith in (by adherence to and reliance on and

complete trust in the Son of God, Who loved me and gave Himself up for me. " Galatians 2:19-20 (AB).

For the apostle Paul, the regime of the faith comes to sound the death knell to the regime of the Law. It places under our eyes the most obvious contrast between these two governances:

"And that means that anyone who tries to live by his own effort, independent of God, is doomed to failure. Scripture backs this up: "Utterly cursed is every person who fails to carry out every detail written in the Book of the law. " The obvious impossibility of carrying out such a moral program should make it plain that no one can sustain a relationship with God that way. The person who lives in right relationship with God does it by embracing what God arranges for him. Doing things for God is the opposite of entering into what God does for you. Habakkuk had it right: "The person who believes God, is set right by God — and that's the real life. " Rule-keeping does not naturally evolve into living by faith, but only perpetuates itself in more and more rule-keeping, a fact observed in Scripture: "The one who does these things [rule-keeping] continues to live by them. " Christ redeemed us from that

self-defeating, cursed life by absorbing it completely into himself. " Galatians 3:10-13 (TM)

Now, we depend on the faith in order to live, and this faith finds its origin in the Word of Christ. This faith is not only true on the day we accept Christ in our life, but at each moment we live by it. We can not begin with the faith and end with our own efforts to top it all. Certainly not! Faith alone allows to receive and to perfect in what Christ has already accomplished for us. His life reigns in us and produces in us the faith that can keep us. In that regard, the apostle Paul would not have been more clear and more scathing, as he wrote to the Galatians:

"Oh, foolish Galatians! Who has cast an evil spell on you? For the meaning of Jesus Christ's death was made as clear to you as if you had seen a picture of his death on the cross. Let me ask you this one question: Did you receive the Holy Spirit by obeying the law of Moses? Of course not! You received the Spirit because you believed the message you heard about Christ. How foolish can you be? After starting your Christian lives in the Spirit, why are you now trying to become perfect by your own human effort?" Galatians 3:1-3 (NLT)

So, for Paul, we begin our life in Christ by faith, and it is perfect by faith. We receive all by His grace, and that same grace produces in us the fruits and works of its own. In this same perspective, I would like to open a parenthesis in conclusion to speak of a term very often misunderstood in the Christian context: repentance. Too many times, has been defined as being this: "*You cease doing certain things* 'bad', *to do other things* 'right'". But true repentance is not only a change of works, or cessation of practicing certain things to look to others. Actually, repentance is far more radical than all this: it is a priori a life changing, a change at the very source. To repent means "*to give his life completely and once and for all*" and take "*the life of Christ*" in exchange. Now you draw all your strength in Christ alone, by faith, and you depend entirely upon him; your own life and all your system of good deeds that you had erected to earn your place in heaven, becomes completely obsolete, vain and foolish. Your own source run dry and from now on, you live on the account and the strength of another than yourself: Christ. So your Savior becomes much more for you "*than a good God who once saved you from your sins*", he now takes up all the space and that includes the affection of your heart, the direction of your life and your life itself.

Jesus wants to reveal Himself to each of us as the divine Bridegroom. All the work of the Spirit has only this goal: to glorify Christ Jesus by giving him alone the glory! To do so, the Spirit leads us to live the heavenly realities; he constantly turns our eyes toward the things above. In the next chapter, the height, we will address this last dimension of the love, to raise ourselves up into him to taste into all its fullness.

Chapter 4

The Height

The name who opens the Heavens

"Blessed be the God and Father of our Lord Jesus Christ, who has blessed us with every spiritual blessing in the heavenly places in Christ!" Ephesians 1:3

"and raised us up together, and made us sit together in the heavenly places in Christ Jesus, that in the ages to come He might show the exceeding riches of His grace in His kindness toward us in Christ Jesus." Ephesians 2:6-7

"The name of the Lord is a strong tower; The righteous run to it and are safe." Proverbs 18:10

"The Lord God is my strength; He will make my feet like deer's feet, And He will make me walk on my high hills [...]" Habakkuk 3:19

The image of "height" in the Scripture has always been associated with the habitation of God, and the fact that man could also live there. Thus, he rules over his enemies and this through faith in Jesus' name. It's like a place accessible for the believers, who see the invisible by faith, and who do not look to the visible circumstances of life. This high place of security and insurance, of deliverance from our enemies, is in the name of Jesus himself.

"Nor is there salvation in any other, for there is no other name under heaven given among men by which we must be saved. " Acts 4:12

"Therefore God also has highly exalted Him and given Him the name which is above every name, that at the name of Jesus every knee should bow, of those in heaven, and of those on earth, and of those under the earth. " Philippians 2:9-10

The name Jesus was given to us as a high and safe place, the rock where you can always seek refuge by faith. His immense love has made accessible this precious name above all, for at the cross, we were united with him in his victory over Satan. Through his death, the Holy Spirit wants to reveal the full magnitude of the triumph that Christ exercised over the devil, who held the power of death.

"Inasmuch then as the children have partaken of flesh and blood, He Himself likewise shared in the same, that through death He might destroy him who had the power of death, that is, the devil, and release those who through fear of death were all their lifetime subject to bondage."
Hebrew 2:14-15

The name of Jesus is given to us as a spiritual gateway into these heavenly places, where he stripped our old enemy. The first part of the prayer that Jesus gave us, begins with these words: *"[...]Our Father in heaven, Hallowed be Your name"* (Matthew 6:9). However, the only place sanctified by the Father's presence was symbolized in the Old Testament by the *"altar of sacrifices"*; we know that this altar speaks about the cross of our Lord Jesus Christ, where his blood was shed for us.

"This shall be a continual burnt offering throughout your generations at the door of the tabernacle of meeting before the Lord, where I will meet you to speak with you. And there I will meet with the children of Israel, and the tabernacle shall be sanctified by My glory."
Exodus 29:42-43

The Father has sanctified the name of Jesus, for it is He that fell on his wrath, making it suitable for men to receive his salvation. The name of Jesus reminds to the eyes of the Father, all the work that Christ has accomplished at the cross; the Father sees the blood and so he can approve us in his presence.

"And according to the law almost all things are purified with blood, and without shedding of blood there is no remission. " Hebrew 9:22

All we ask of the Father can only be obtained by the name of Jesus. But this name is not like a label you put on you. This does not work by *"saying the name of Jesus "*. Full faith in Him is required. By faith, we recognize that it is He who has satisfied the demands of the Law and that has reconciled us with the Father. For behind this name hides the whole work of justification and sanctification that was exercised by Jesus and His victory over Satan. For God looks at our heart, and sees if our faith is really placed on the altar of sacrifices, the cross of Christ, the only meeting place with the Father sanctified by his glory. If you do not understand the impact of this work of Christ at the cross, then your faith will remain vegetative, because it does not draw in its roots, where the Father has provided everything. For all the heavenly blessings in Christ was placed into an account which is hidden directly at the cross. This is so because of the express will of the Father, to make this altar a privileged place with your relationship in Him. When you contemplate the cross, the only thing that transpires your own work, is all your transgressions and your sins that have crucified the Son of God. It stays there no reason for human pride or boast about anything whatsoever. Only remains the work of infinite love of God who loved us while to give up, despite our manifest unworthiness. The cross is the only place where human pride finds its own abolition, finally his permanent death.

"Can we boast, then, that we have done anything to be accepted by God? No, because our acquittal is not based on obeying the law. It is based on faith. So we are made right with God through faith and not by obeying the law." Romans 3:27-28 (NLT)

This is how God can begin to manifest his reign, and to accomplish His heavenly will on earth through us, his adopted children.

The Heavens earth-fulfilling

The name of Jesus opens the door in the heavenly places. Heaven comes down to earth because of his name, when it is pronounced in faith and knowledge of all that Christ is for us, all that He did for us on the cross. This propels us in him, in his own person, at the same place where he now resides, that is to say, in the heavenly places. For we must realize that the spirit knows no limitations restricted to our body. The apostle Paul was so aware of the fact that he did not even feel the need to be in person, in body, in the midst of the Corinthians, to settle some matters:

"For I indeed, as absent in body but present in spirit, have already judged (as though I were present) him who has so done this deed. In the name of our Lord Jesus Christ, when you are gathered together, along with my spirit, with the power of our Lord Jesus Christ, deliver such a one to Satan for the destruction of the flesh, that his spirit may be saved in the day of the Lord Jesus. "
I Corinthians 5.3-5

Indeed, if we have become a single plant with Christ because of his death upon the cross, this union is also manifested in our reign with him in the heavenly places. The contact between us and Christ is not only a radio contact, it is not only that communication was restored between us and Christ. But it is a contact of spirit with spirit; a part of me, the spirit, becomes really present in Christ in the heavenly places. This becomes a relationship of love altogether personal, for the spirit is the essence of our being. In us the spirit is this unmaterial entity and therefore not restricted to the physical realm. The following verses describe not a future reality, but an already accomplished fact:

"giving thanks to the Father who has qualified us to be partakers of the inheritance of the saints in the light. He has delivered us from the power of darkness and conveyed us into the kingdom of the Son of His love. " Colossians 1:12-13

All these things are already accomplished and accessible for us. The Inheritance is already available, since death has struck our King and his name has now become the signature of His will. When a person comes to Christ, he or she is invited to enter the four foundations of grace, and it is at the altar of the cross that they discover them. While his inheritance is hidden there, all that Heaven has in store for us call to be discovered. It is like "the branch of the Heavenly Bank" where you can go collect all that Christ has already deposited in our joint account. This is of course just an image, but it reflects the reality provided at the cross where the divine joins earth.

"I will betroth you to Me in faithfulness, And you shall know the Lord. "It shall come to pass in that day that I will answer," says the Lord; "I will answer the heavens, And they shall answer the earth. The earth shall answer with grain, With new wine, And with oil; They shall answer Jezreel. Then I will sow her for Myself in the earth, And I will have mercy on her who had not obtained mercy; Then I will say to those who were not My people, 'You are My people!' And they shall say, 'You are my God!'" Hosea 2.20-23

The cross is the meeting place of God with man, where heaven touches the earth. In itself, the cross carries these four dimensions that are spread starting from its center, Christ crucified:

- the *horizontal dimension* of the cross — which designates the width and the length of God's love;

- and the *vertical dimension* — which under-
lies the depth and the height.

But there is a divine order; God does not answer
the land first, but first of all the heavens. In other
words, you must go to the heavens in Jesus Christ
in order to receive from him what he already
accomplished. This is why Jesus ordered to "[...]
*seek first the kingdom of God and His
righteousness, and all these things shall be added
to you"* (Matthew 6:33); By seeking for your own
fulfillment or according to your will, you will go
nowhere and you will find yourself out of the
benefits of grace. God does not listen the selfish
prayers. He answers prayers only centered on
Christ and his kingdom. In Christ is found all the
heavenly blessings (Ephesians 1:3); we must
learn to remain and live there. The only and true
gateway to the Kingdom of God is the cross.

It is a little like, throughout our lives, God was
asking us to share continually of Jesus' death,
burial and resurrection. Contrary to the opinion
of certain persons in connection with the cross,
sharing his death for us is the source of all the
blessings; it's just entering what he has
accomplished for us through his death. They

identify themselves with his death, acknow-
ledging that it is our sins that brought him there,
but it is also to recognize that there, all our sins
are washed away forever, in their inherent nature
and their consequences. To share his burial is
even more difficult for many christians; it is to
accept to remain there in his presence, in the
heavenly places until his power is made on us. It
belongs to Him alone to lift us up, when He may
think fit. In this waiting time, of tests and trials of
faith, some begin to doubt and prefer to go back
to their daily occupation.

For the identification to His death represents our
exodus from Egypt, and that was in itself
something glorious and liberating. But the
identification with his burial is represented by the
desert, where nothing natural can live on its own
resources. This time of wilderness is necessary
and ordained by God, before fully experiencing
the identification with his resurrection. For the
resurrection is represented by our entrance into
the promised land. In this wilderness, the danger
to complain, to murmur, or tempt God reached its
highest level. It is then that we can be pushed to
think that this phase represents a divine
punishment, but it is quite the opposite. It is the

place that brings us closest to our blessing, because it allows the character of Christ to develop in us.

The desert can not be a punishment, for Christ has already carried on himself at the cross the punishment of all our sins. God allows our lives in the wilderness for the same reason that he has allowed the Son of God to remain in the grave. The enemy had to be defeated completely, in its lower spheres of darkness and to its highest places of domination. The burial allowed the Spirit of Christ to visit these places, to get out more victorious and triumphant. We can not defeat the enemy unless we destroy its nerve center. We need to go in the heart of his fortress, if we want to disarm him. Jesus came out of hell with the keys of death in his hands, having stripped the one who had authority over death, that is to say, the devil.

" Having disarmed principalities and powers, He made a public spectacle of them, triumphing over them in it. " Colossians 2:15

"I am He who lives, and was dead, and behold, I am alive forevermore. Amen. And I have the keys of Hades (hell) and of Death. " Revelation 1:18

Thus in our identification with his burial, we too emerge as a victor over the devil, our great enemy forever. However, the time in the wilderness will be a place of training and self-denial. In the Old Covenant, the wilderness has lasted forty years since the heart of the people had not yet received the true circumcision. In the New Covenant, the wilderness only lasted fifty days, which is why, already at Pentecost, the power of the resurrection of Christ has been pouring on the apostles. So it will be for us if we approach all that Christ has accomplished toward us at the cross. The union with Christ and the taking possession of the four foundations acquired at the cross, provide us unhindered access in the presence of God. The Scripture must take back all its rights in our lives and prevail in all its splendor, before producing the fruit of the resurrection. In fact, it is the first thing that Jesus implemented in his disciples, before he shared to them his power of resurrection.

"And He opened their understanding, that they might comprehend the Scriptures. Then He said to them, "Thus it is written, and thus it was necessary for the Christ to suffer and to rise from the dead the third day, and that repentance and remission of sins should be preached in His name to all nations,

beginning at Jerusalem. And you are witnesses of these things. Behold, I send the Promise of My Father upon you; but tarry in the city of Jerusalem until you are endued with power from on high. " "
Luke 24:45-49

The fire that destroys the devil's work

In our identification with his resurrection, the new life of the Spirit, we also participate in his reign; *"[...] He might destroy the works of the devil "* (I John 3:8) is a part of it also. By his Spirit, we can therefore commune at his table and reign with him over the enemy. Such a reality is still demonstrated on the altar, by the sacrifice of Christ at the cross. The expiatory sacrifice of two goats symbolized each of the first works of Christ at the cross: the justification that manifests the width of his love and the sanctification which demonstrates the length. We have also seen that the fat of the expiatory goat burned on the altar, foreshadowed the energy resources of Christ became ours through communion with his sacrifice. His Spirit was going to be poured out on us so to perfect the depth of his love in us all. Finally, a last element of the expiatory goat had to also be executed to raise us with him over the acting powers of darkness in this world.

"The bull for the sin offering and the goat for the sin offering, whose blood was brought in to make atonement in the Holy Place, shall be carried outside the camp. And they shall burn in the fire their skins, their flesh, and their offal." Leviticus 16:27

"We have an altar from which those who serve the tabernacle have no right to eat. For the bodies of those animals, whose blood is brought into the sanctuary by the high priest for sin, are burned outside the camp. Therefore Jesus also, that He might sanctify the people with His own blood, suffered outside the gate. Therefore let us go forth to Him, outside the camp, bearing His reproach. For here we have no continuing city, but we seek the one to come." Hebrew 13:10-14

If Jesus went outside the camp, it was First of all to bring the destruction in the enemy's camp. The skin, the flesh and the feces of these animals speak to us of all the weight of shame and mockery that Christ endured from the devil. In dying, he has like started a fire of God inside of the enemy's camp to its destruction. A figure of this is given to us in the Old Testament through the history of the strong man, Samson. Although this last one had few of the characters of Christ, what he has experienced provides us with a likeness of the One who was to come: Christ, the real strong man, that was going to have victory over the devil.

Let us observe some analogies between Christ and Samson, that puts in the foreground a messianic type:

- Samson's birth is announced by an angel (Judges 13:3) — as also for Jesus (Luke 1:31);

- this chils will be " *consecrated to God* " or *"Nazarite "* (Judges 13:7) — Jesus was consacreted to God from childhood (Luke 1:35) and called *"Nazareth "* (Acts 6:14);

- Samson was covered with a prodigious superhuman physical strength (Judges 16:5) — Jesus, likewise, expelled out demons because on him rested divine strength (Luke 4:14);

- Samson was the only judge to stay directly in enemy territory, battling alone without an army (Judges 16:1-4) — as well, Jesus came and lived here on earth to defeat the prince of this world and he was to fight the battle alone (I John 3:8);

- Samson was also the only one to kill more enemies by his death than during his entire life (Judges 16:30) — likewise, Jesus by his death has done more harm to the enemy throughout his life, completely destroying his works at the cross (Colossians 2:15);

- Samson was the only one of those of the Old Testament, to offer himself voluntarily to death for the cause of God (Judges 16:28-30) — similarly, Jesus willingly sacrificed himself for his sheep (John 10:17-18);

- Samson's death was caused by the betrayal of someone who was eating at his table (Judges 16:4,19) — as well Jesus was going to be put to death by the treachery of one of those that was eating with him at the table: Judas Iscariot (Jean 13:18).

The Gospel of John describes this journey of Jesus. First, he was to face directly the prince of this world by supporting these taunts, and then bring down upon himself the divine judgment.

"I will no longer talk much with you, for the ruler of this world is coming, and he has nothing in Me. " John 14:30

"Now is the judgment of this world; now the ruler of this world will be cast out. " John 12:31

"And when He (the Comforter) has come, He will convict the world of sin, and of righteousness, and of judgment: of sin. because they do not believe in Me; of righteousness, because I go to My Father and you see Me no more; of judgment, because the ruler of this world is judged. " John 16:8-11

Christ was holy, separated from the world, completely opposite in nature to the prince of this world, Satan. At his death, even if it was a dead body that has been transported to the tomb, his body still had more power and authority than all the united powers of this world. For this body was holy; the weakness of God is stronger than the strength of this world. Death could not hold captive the Son of God, God's fire illuminated even within the grave.

"[This is] because the foolish thing [that has its source in] God is wiser than men, and the weak thing [that springs] from God is stronger than men. " I Corinthians 1:25 (AB)

The apostle Paul explains why it could not be otherwise:

" Now this I say, brethren, that flesh and blood cannot inherit the kingdom of God ; nor does corruption inherit incorruption." I Corinthians 15:50

Even if the body of Jesus has suffered our punishment and that he has died carrying our sin, his own flesh was not affected by sin. Even in the grave, it proved impossible that corruption reaches him, for he had remained holy and blameless. This is what the apostle Peter also resumes in his first speech at Pentecost:

"whom God raised up, having loosed the pains of death, because it was not possible that He should be held by it. For David says concerning Him: 'I foresaw the Lord always before my face, For He is at my right hand, that I may not

be shaken.Therefore my heart rejoiced, and my tongue was glad ; Moreover my flesh also will rest in hope. For You will not leave my soul in Hades (hell), Nor will You allow Your Holy One to see corruption. '" Acts 2:24-27

There could not be decomposition of the flesh of Jesus, as there was in it something incorruptible, not being affected by the sin.

"Therefore He also says in another Psalm: 'You will not allow Your Holy One to see corruption. ' "For David, after he had served his own generation by the will of God, fell asleep, was buried with his fathers, and saw corruption; but He whom God raised up saw no corruption. " Acts 13:35-37

So, the divine fire only could raised him as saint and new breed, henceforth, Jesus would become the one not only that baptizes of the Spirit, but also of fire.

"Therefore being exalted to the right hand of God, and having received from the Father the promise of the Holy Spirit, He poured out this which you now see and hear. " Acts 2:33

"[...] He will baptize you with the Holy Spirit and fire." Luke 3:16

"Then there appeared to them divided tongues, as of fire, and one sat upon each of them. And they were all filled with the Holy Spirit and began to speak with other tongues, as the Spirit gave them utterance." Acts 2:3-4

Take note that the fire still has a dual property; for the wicked, it is destructive because he is compared with straw in the Scriptures (Psaumes 37:1-2). For the righteous, the fire can not reach him; instead of consuming him, it only purify and make him even stronger and radiant (Malachi 3.2-3). This is what happened to Christ and this is what is happening to us too, when we carry his nature in us by faith in his work at the cross.

The highest portion of the Inheritance
"O Lord, You are the portion of my inheritance and my cup; You maintain my lot. The lines have fallen to me in pleasant places; Yes, I have a good inheritance. I will bless the Lord who has given me counsel; My heart also instructs me in the night seasons. I have set the Lord always before me; Because He is at my right hand I shall not be moved. Therefore my heart is glad, and my

glory rejoices; My flesh also will rest in hope. "
Psalm 16:5-9

The most beautiful and precious part of our inheritance culminates in the presence of our Bridegroom. More than the glory or the richness, more than the victory over Satan, the person of Jesus himself meets all requirements and fills the heart to make him perfectly happy. All his love finds its source and its apogee at the cross where the Son of God has triumphed over all our enemies.

"which He worked in Christ when He raised Him from the dead and seated Him at His right hand in the heavenly places, far above all principality and power and might and dominion, and every name that is named, not only in this age but also in that which is to come. And He put all things under His feet, and gave Him to be head over all things to the church, which is His body, the fullness of Him who fills all in all. " Ephesians 1:20-23

God loved us so highly, that he has designed to elevate us with Christ in an authority and a dignity that are not ours. His royal largesse has made us participant of his nature and of his Spirit, but now his majesty made us sit on the very throne of Christ.

"and raised us up together, and made us sit together in the heavenly places in Christ Jesus." Ephesians 2:6

All these things are accessible through faith, and they become reality for those who have become used to take refuge daily in the name of Jesus, into intimate communion with Him. We must draw our strength in him, always keeping our spirit alert in prayer and in a continual dependency on the Holy Spirit.

"And do not be drunk with wine, in which is dissipation; but be filled with the Spirit, speaking to one another in psalms and hymns and spiritual songs, singing and making melody in your heart to the Lord, giving thanks always for all things to God the Father in the name of our Lord Jesus Christ." Ephesiens 5:18-20

"Finally, my brethren, be strong in the Lord and in the power of His might." Ephesians 6:10

The more we respond positively to the divine love in every dimension, the more God himself manifests that love in our lives and multiplies it. What did the apostle Paul a servant so fruitful is that his heart had been seized by God and, in turn, he wanted to capture the heart of God.

"Not that I have already attained, or am already perfected; but I press on, that I may lay hold of that for which Christ Jesus has also laid hold of me. " Philippians 3:12

In the same sense, the prophet Jeremiah said:

"Your words were found, and I ate them, And Your word was to me the joy and rejoicing of my heart; For I am called by Your name, O Lord God of hosts. " Jeremiah 15:16

"O Lord, You induced me, and I was persuaded; You are stronger than I, and have prevailed [...]" Jeremiah 20:7

Do not let the love of God pass on, without grasping it! It is not because God is love we can afford to neglect it by letting ourselves be absorbed by our daily activities. His love invites us to follow and produced such a ripple effect, that we must act like fools not to take hold of it. By neglecting such great salvation and abusing his grace, we mock God and we may pay dearly for it.

"Do not be deceived, God is not mocked; for whatever a man sows, that he will also reap."
Galatians 6:7

If we do not learn now, to take refuge in Jesus continually, while things are going relatively well, what will happen tomorrow? When nobody can buy or sell without the mark of the beast (Revelation 13.17), it may be too late to begin to trust in God. Learn to depend on Him now for our daily needs, so we will not be surprised as by a thief in the midst of the night.

All the greatness of His love leads us to come ever closer to Him, so we too may become like Him, a channel of love for others. In Him, all becomes possible, for He has promised himself to walk with us.

"[...] The Lord is with you while you are with Him. If you seek Him, He will be found by you; but if you forsake Him, He will forsake you."
II Chronicles 15:2

"Draw near to God and He will draw near to you [...]" James 4:8

The grace manifests itself with boundless generosity, but does not like to be despised or considered as insignificant crumbs.

Jesus displayed a love without measure and at the same time, he demanded of his disciples an exclusive and unreservedly commitment.

"He who loves father or mother more than Me is not worthy of Me. And he who loves son or daughter more than Me is not worthy of Me." Matthew 10:37

So let us appreciate the true value of the greatness of divine love, and to recognize the very legitimate rights He enjoys over us.

Since He has paid in blood for the authenticity of His love, it is right and proper to give Him first place in our hearts He deserves it.

"Grace be with all those who love our Lord Jesus Christ in sincerity. Amen." Ephesians 6:24

Conclusion

When God commands to love, is it really a commandment? Is it hard to love when we are deeply and passionately in love? But this is the kind of love that God loves us with. The divine love, called in Greek "*Agape*", is far from being devoid of feeling. God himself appears as a "*consuming fire*" (Hebrew 12:29), which "*Its flames are flames of fire, a most vehement flame*" (Song of Solomon 8:6). He loves us so profoundly that he is jealous of us (James 4:5), in such a way that he desires not to share this intimacy with anyone else.

How much we want to know the full extent of his love, an impact on our lives that can only produce a radical transformation of our way of being, thinking and acting. Let us remember always that at the cross was the ultimate act of his love manifested to us. There, *in the first implement*, he unveiled his incomparable largesses, the divine King gave his life in sacrifice so that to be introduced to thine, by delivering us forever from sin and its corrupted nature. He has recreated in himself a new humanity of which he became the leader, making us part of his own divine nature. For all this, he paid a huge price: that of his own death at the cross in an unprecedented outburst of love down here.

In the second implement, our God of love extended the reach of his work, also taking on himself all the long list of tragic consequences of our sins. He suffered in himself our separation from God: broken because of our iniquities, bruised because of our sicknesses, chastised due to our transgressions, humiliated because of our shame, condemned because of our guilt. His soul and his body have suffered the worst torments, so that the trace left by our sin disappear forever. No one, neither Father God nor man nor devil can in recall the least memory, for Christ washed away all the negative reports which subsisted against us. Incomparable love of a God so great, that comes to bear on him the chastisement merited by children! What forbearance! Now we, his adopted children, are integrated into his own plan of blessings; the blessing due to the perfect life of Christ become ours.

In the third implement, divine love has attacked the book that have doomed us. Nevertheless, this book of the Law originated from God himself, but he did not have the desired results. Instead of giving life as planned, he instead procured death. This is how God has decided, according to his deep wisdom, we are now placed under the exclusive custody of his Spirit. What precision into the details the Spirit would he allow in our lives! What gentleness and fingering characterize the spiritual depth of his love! His Spirit takes care of us more tenderly than a mother would with her child. But for this regime change to be possible, from the governance of the Law to the stewardship of the Spirit, it had first to come Jesus Christ accomplish the Law perfectly. Then, in his death, he has identified us with him to subtract us from this Law. Having died with Him at the cross, we are now free to belong to Christ, and benefit from the tender cares of the Holy Spirit.

Finally, in the fourth implement, God fills up his love, by lowering himself to us, to raise us unto him. He unites us with him in his reign, made us sit down by his side on the throne of Christ, and sets us above all authorities and all powers in the heavenly places. Again, it is the cross that manifests the height of his love, where he delivered himself the battle for us. He triumphed over Satan and snatched the keys of death and of hell. From miserable, from lost and from slave that we were, he transported us into the kingdom of his Son, even higher than the angels. Now having become our heavenly Bridegroom, he place on the head of the Bride that was unworthy, an uncorruptible crown of glory. O grace of pure love from our wonderful God, that has opened wide his arms to welcome his prodigal children !

What largesse !
The Lamb has paid with his separation from God the weight of our sin.

What longanimity !
The Lamb has suffered by his own death the wages of our sin.

What depth !
The Lamb took his own people with him in his death to release them forever from the power of the Law.

What height !

The Lamb has fought till the blood to break down the devil's power over us, and rise us with him forever in the heavenly places.

"Now when He had taken the scroll, the four living creatures and the twenty-four elders fell down before the Lamb, each having a harp, and golden bowls full of incense, which are the prayers of the saints. And they sang a new song, saying: 'You are worthy to take the scroll, And to open its seals; For You were slain, And have redeemed us to God by Your blood Out of every tribe and tongue and people and nation, And have made us kings and priests to our God; And we shall reign on the earth.' Then I looked, and I heard the voice of many angels around the throne, the living creatures, and the elders; and the number of them was ten thousand times ten thousand, and thousands of thousands, saying with a loud voice: 'Worthy is the Lamb who was slain to receive power and riches and wisdom, And strength and honor and glory and blessing!'" Revelation 5:8-12

Amen!

(so be it!)

—End—

To be published

by the same author

www.JeromePouliot.com

The Crowned Horns Of The Lamb's Power

A divine revelation about the power of the horns from the two altars in God's Temple: Christ and Him crucified.

Éditions
Sous Tes Ailes

www.EditionsSousTesAiles.com

(Under Your Wings House Publishing)

www.ingramcontent.com/pod-product-compliance
Lightning Source LLC
Chambersburg PA
CBHW022027090426
42739CB00006BA/315